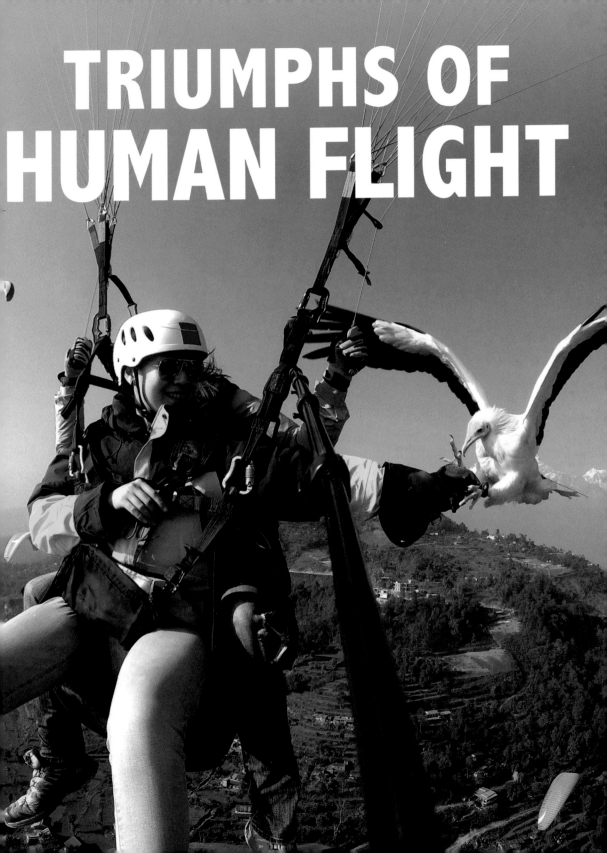

TRIUMPHS OF HUMAN FLIGHT

Thanks to the creative team:
Senior Editor: Alice Peebles
Fact Checking: Tom Jackson
Picture Research: Nic Dean
Design: 38a The Shop

Hungry Tomato®
A division of Lerner Publishing Group, Inc.
241 First Avenue North
Minneapolis, MN 55401 USA

For reading levels and more information, look up this title at
www.lernerbooks.com.

Main body text set in Avenir Next Condensed 12/14.

Library of Congress Cataloging-in-Publication Data

Names: Harris, Tim, 1957- author.
Title: Triumphs of human flight : from wingsuits to parachutes / Tim Harris.
Description: Minneapolis, MN : Hungry Tomato, [2018] | Series: Feats
    of flight | Audience: Ages 8–12. | Audience: Grades 4 to 6. | Includes
    bibliographical references and index.
Identifiers: LCCN 2017060219 (print) | LCCN 2017057007 (ebook) | ISBN
    9781541523845 (eb pdf) | ISBN 9781541500969 (lb : alk. paper)
Subjects: LCSH: Flying-machines–Technological innovations–Juvenile
    literature. | Skydiving–Juvenile literature. | Gliders (Aeronautics)–Juvenile
    literature. | Personal propulsion units–Juvenile literature. | Ballooning–
    Juvenile literature.
Classification: LCC TL600 (print) | LCC TL600 .H37 2018 (ebook) | DDC
    629.1/4–dc23

LC record available at https://lccn.loc.gov/2017060219

Manufactured in the United States of America
1-43765-33625-3/6/2018

TRIUMPHS OF HUMAN FLIGHT

by Tim Harris

HUNGRY
TOMATO®

Minneapolis

Charles County Public Library
La Plata Branch
301-934-9001 301-870-3520
www.ccplonline.org

CONTENTS

LOOK, NO ENGINE

Think what it would be like to rise up into the clouds in a basket beneath a colorful balloon. Imagine cruising high over the countryside in an aircraft powered by nothing more than the sun's energy. And what would it be like to pedal a plane along a runway and up into the air? These aren't imaginary flying machines from a storybook—they really do exist.

No fossil fuels

While they are all different, these aircraft have one thing in common: none of them rely on **fossil fuels**, such as diesel and gas. Fossil fuels come from oil buried deep below Earth's surface, and they won't last forever. Also, when fossil fuels are burned in engines, they produce a **greenhouse gas** called carbon dioxide. As this builds up in Earth's **atmosphere**, it makes the climate warmer. This is called **climate change**.

▶ *A hang glider pilot floats high above the shore, kept afloat by a large fabric wing.*

Gravity and air resistance

Just because the air is invisible doesn't mean there's nothing there. Earth's atmosphere is packed full of tiny particles, or molecules, of gas. They are too small to see, but they create air resistance. This force opposes the force of gravity that pulls objects toward Earth. It is air resistance that makes a parachute descend gradually, for example. As a large open parachute falls, it meets far more air resistance than the relatively small parachute does. This allows both parachute and person to descend slowly.

The rounded shape of the parachute helps to keep it balanced.

Ropes safely attach the person to the parachute.

The parachute's large surface area helps create air resistance.

The force of gravity pulls the person to the ground.

The force of gravity is counteracted by the force of air resistance from the parachute.

Cleaner, greener, cheaper

The alternatives to aircraft powered by fossil fuels are cleaner, and many are cheaper too. These craft rely on wind, warm air currents, or the power of the sun to get from place to place. Some are intended purely for fun, but others could be used to transport passengers in the future. Read on to find out more.

PARACHUTES

When a parachute opens, it creates air resistance. It is this that allows people to jump from aircraft and land safely on the ground thousands of feet below. Parachutes are used by pilots escaping from damaged planes, by **relief missions** dropping food parcels to people suffering famine, or most often just for fun!

Suppose you fell from a plane without a parachute. It's a scary thought: your body would zoom through the air like a stone. By opening a parachute strapped to your back, you greatly increase air resistance and this slows you down. You drift to the ground safely, more like a feather than a stone. Parachutes are made of light, strong material—usually nylon.

Ripcord

▲ *The parachute is opened by pulling on a release mechanism called a ripcord.*

Letting rip

If someone jumped from a plane with the parachute already open, it would get tangled up with the aircraft. This would be dangerous for the jumper and might even cause the plane to crash. So the parachute is packed on the jumper's back, and they open it only when clear of the plane.

Parachutists jump from a plane. They haven't yet opened their chutes.

Shapes

Different parachute designs have different uses.

The circular parachute has been used by the military since World War I and is the oldest type.

The cruciform design (a modifed T-11 shown here) reduces side-to-side swing as a parachutist comes down, providing a more comfortable descent.

The ram-air parachute has two layers of fabric connected by "ribs" to form cells, or compartments. Unlike circular and cruciform designs, it is capable of **lift** and popular with sports parachutists.

WINGSUITS

Imagine your excitement as you wait for the signal to jump from a plane thousands of feet above the countryside. On your back you have a fabric wingsuit and a parachute. The wingsuit is stretched between your legs, and between your arms and body. Suddenly, the light in front of you flashes from red to green– the signal to jump. You leap through the hatch with your arms and legs outstretched. What a feeling!

Even without an engine, you fly through the air at tremendous speed. Your descent is slowed by the wingsuit, but you are thankful for your protective helmet and nylon bodysuit. After a minute or two you realize you are falling, so you pull the ripcord and release the parachute. Now you can drift slowly and safely to the ground.

Flying from a cliff

Wingsuit flyers don't have to jump from planes. Some leap from the top of a cliff or mountain with their arms and legs outstretched. They still have a parachute attached, so after the first few seconds of freefall flight, they can slow their descent to the ground.

These flyers are jumping in the Dolomite mountains in Italy. They spread their wingsuits as they leap.

Batsuits

Wingsuits increase the flyer's surface area and air resistance. But although these "batsuits" reduce the speed of fall, they can't keep a flyer airborne for very long. Different parts of a wingsuit act like parts of a plane. The arms are like the wings of a plane, the fabric between the legs provides stability, and movements of the head control the pilot's flying direction.

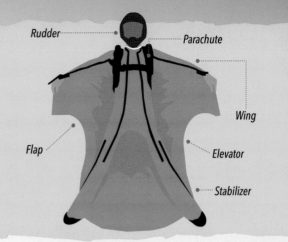

Rudder

Parachute

Wing

Flap

Elevator

Stabilizer

▲ Four wingsuit flyers moving in formation

HUMAN POWER

For centuries, people have tried to fly planes with their own muscle power. Not many have succeeded! Many designs have been tried, but the big problem was always the weight of the aircraft. Large wings and forward motion were needed to keep the craft in the air, but large wings are heavy and no one was strong enough to keep the planes moving forward for more than a few seconds.

The invention of strong, ultra-light materials changed all that. The Daedalus 88 has a skeleton of **carbon fiber** tubes and a "skin" of lightweight plastic. It weighs just 71 pounds (32 kg), about the same as a ten-year-old boy.

Cycling to France

Just after dawn one fine morning in June 1979, champion cyclist Bryan Allan sat in the **cockpit** of the lightweight Gossamer Albatross plane and cycled furiously. The Albatross's propeller turned as he pedaled along a runway and lifted into the air. He passed over the coast and out over the open waters of the English Channel. Three hours later he had cycled the plane 22 miles (36 km) to France–and into the record books.

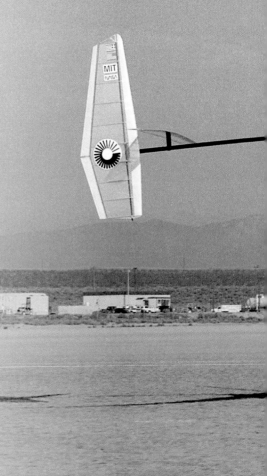

▲ *Gossamer Albatross was the first human-powered plane to cross the English Channel.*

Glorious failures

"Birdman" competitions are organized every year. People build their own planes and attempt to fly them—without the help of an engine. Some of the designs are very funny!

▶ *This plane crashed straight into the sea.*

▲ *In 1988, Olympic cyclist Kanellos Kanellopoulos cycled Daedalus 88 over the sea between the Greek islands of Crete and Santorini, creating the record for the longest pedal-powered aircraft flight—72 miles (115 km).*

GLIDERS

As you sail high above green hills and trees, the only sound you can hear is the air whooshing past the cockpit. You are flying in a glider and it's fun! Glider flight is a clean, quiet, relaxing way of seeing the world. Although it doesn't have an engine, a glider can stay in the air for hours and fly great distances.

A glider is a heavier-than-air aircraft. There is no engine, and the pilot has to use their skill and the weather conditions to remain airborne. A modern, high-performance glider is built from **fiberglass**. It has long, thin wings and a narrow **fuselage**. This means there is very little air resistance, or drag, as the glider moves through the sky.

Riding a thermal

An experienced glider pilot looks for signs of rising columns of air, or thermals. Once the glider reaches the thermal, the rising air will carry it higher. On a warm, sunny day there may be many thermals, which will keep a glider airborne for several hours and carry it hundreds of miles.

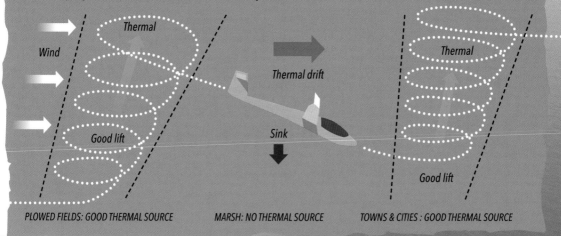

Wind

Thermal

Good lift

Thermal drift

Sink

Thermal

Good lift

PLOWED FIELDS: GOOD THERMAL SOURCE   MARSH: NO THERMAL SOURCE   TOWNS & CITIES : GOOD THERMAL SOURCE

Launch!

Gliders are launched in two ways. Some are towed behind a powered plane and are only released once they are high above the ground. This is called an aerotowing. Other gliders are launched from the ground after being pulled along a runway at speed by a cable.

▲ A small powered plane tows a glider at the end of a cable. When the glider has gained height, the cable will be released and the glider fly without help.

▲ A pilot's-eye view from the cockpit of a glider as it flies over a town

▲ Gliders can travel long distances—
if the weather conditions are good.

HANG GLIDERS

LEADING EDGE TUBE

You may have seen multi-colored hang gliders performing amazing tricks in the air over a hillside. Their arrow-shaped wings seem to flit backward and forward on the breeze. Hang glider pilots launch their craft by taking a running jump off the edge of a steep hill. Then they skillfully **maneuver** so they catch the wind to stay in the air.

HARNESS

FLIGHT BAG

Riding thermals

Once airborne, a skilled hang glider pilot can sail through the air to find updrafts of warm air called thermals, which lift the craft higher. By "hopping" from thermal to thermal, a hang glider can stay in the air for hours. An American named Dustin Martin once flew 475 miles (764 km) across Texas before having to land.

▲ A hang glider flyer takes a run-up before launching from the side of a hill.

The pilot of this hang glider can direct the craft to the left or right by pushing down on the left or right end of the control bar.

A hang glider pilot performs an aerial maneuver.

ALUMINIUM FRAME

POLYESTER FIBER SAIL

CONTROL BAR

The hang glider itself is a lightweight machine with an **aluminium** frame supporting a wing made of a **synthetic** fiber called polyester. The flyer is suspended in a harness hanging from the frame. He or she can make the hang glider go left or right simply by moving their body.

Useful variometer

The display on a gadget called a variometer tells a hang glider pilot if the air around the craft is rising or falling. This information is very important because rising air will lift the hang glider and keep it airborne. The pilot uses the variometer to find the middle of a thermal and gain maximum height.

SOLAR POWER

Solar-powered planes may be the future for "clean" flight. They use energy cells, called photovoltaic cells, to convert the sun's rays into electricity. This powers motors that turn propellers to drive the plane forward. Solar-powered technology doesn't produce pollution, unlike aircraft fueled by diesel and gas.

Solar Impulse 2

Until recently, solar power couldn't keep a plane in the sky for long or when flying at night. The amazing technology used in Solar Impulse 2 changed all this. In 2016, this solar-powered craft was the first to travel around the world. On one leg of its journey, pilot André Borschberg flew nonstop from Japan to Hawaii, across the Pacific Ocean, in five days and nights. This flight set a new record for the longest solo flight in an airplane of any kind.

▲ The long wings and thin fuselage of Solar Impulse 2 are designed to make the plane light and buoyant.

SOLARIMPULSE
AROUND THE WORLD

Flying at night

The ultralight carbon-fiber wings of Solar Impulse 2 need to be long enough to house thousands of photovoltaic cells. In fact, the wings are as long as those of an Airbus A380, the world's largest passenger airliner, but they are no heavier than a large car!

▲ To save energy, Solar Impulse's cockpit is not heated.

◄ In 2001, the solar-powered Helios aircraft reached an altitude of 31,247 feet (9,524 m). This was a world record for a plane not powered by rockets.

Photovoltaic cells

When sunlight shines on a photovoltaic cell, it generates an electric current. This can be stored in a battery or used to drive an electric motor. Solar Impulse has more than 17,000 photovoltaic cells. During the day when the sun is shining, they produce more electricity than needed to power the plane. The excess is stored in batteries and released to drive the motors at night.

▲ Energy from photovoltaic cells enabled Solar Impulse to fly in two legs over the Pacific Ocean.

BALLOONS

The first hot-air balloons were made in China nearly 2,000 years ago, but it wasn't until 1783 that the French Montgolfier brothers built a balloon that could carry passengers. The first passengers were a sheep, a duck, and a rooster!

A balloon is one of the simplest flying machines. It has two main parts: a fabric **envelope** filled with gas, and a basket hanging beneath it to carry passengers or equipment. For the balloon to fly, the air in the envelope has to be lighter than the air surrounding it, so it rises. Some balloons are filled with a lighter-than-air gas such as helium. Most are filled with ordinary air that is heated to make it lighter.

▼ With their burners firing, three balloons are about to take off.

▲ The sky is filled with multicolored balloons at the annual Albuquerque International Balloon Fiesta in New Mexico.

Record-breakers

Modern balloons can fly great distances and climb to amazing heights. In March 1999, Breitling Orbiter 3 was the first to fly around the world nonstop, in just under 20 days. The Indian balloonist Vijaypat Singhania took his hot-air balloon to far more than twice the height of Mount Everest. In 2015, Troy Bradley and Leonid Tiukhtyaev flew their helium balloon across the Pacific Ocean from Japan to Mexico—an amazing 5,261 miles (8,467 km).

The lower part of the balloon is made from a fire-resistant material, so it doesn't catch fire when the burner flares.

Parachute valve

Envelope

Skirt

Burners

Wind guard

Wicker basket

Balloon burner

The balloon pilot starts the burner to get the balloon to lift off, or when it needs to gain height during its flight. A pilot light **ignites** a mixture of **propane** and air, producing a flame. The flame heats the air in the balloon envelope, causing it to rise. Once the balloon is aloft, the burner can be switched off.

FUN BALLOONS

Every year festivals are organized around the world to show off the amazing colors and shapes of hot-air balloons–and to race them against each other.

Balloonists often try to break records. In 2017, 85 multicolored hot-air balloons flew together across the English Channel. One of the most amazing of these festivals is the Albuquerque International Balloon Fiesta in New Mexico. Hundreds of fun hot-air balloons are flown there. Many are shaped like cartoon characters, animals, or cacti. Elsewhere, balloons are illuminated and flown after dark. Others "dance" in the sky to music.

THE FUTURE

Planes that do not have fuel-burning engines are not as powerful as those that do. Unlike jet airliners, "clean" aircraft can't carry hundreds of passengers thousands of miles. They do not have the **endurance**. This is a problem scientists and engineers are working on.

Hybrid technology

One solution is hybrid technology. In a hybrid **airship**, most of the lift is provided by the airship's lighter-than-air helium gas, and dynamic lift is also produced by the aircraft's unique shape as it moves through air. The Lockheed LM1 hybrid airship can carry heavy loads and passengers to places where there are no airstrips. It is ideal for getting supplies into remote areas quickly, for example, if people need emergency medical supplies. The LM1 is filled with helium to keep it airborne, but it has diesel-fueled engines to drive it forward.

▲ The Airlander 10 airship can carry 11 tons (10 t) of cargo. Its "big brother," Airlander 50, will be able to lift 55 tons (50 t) in its 17,650-ft^3 (500-m^3) cargo hold when it is built in the 2020s.

Hydrogen cells

Another alternative may be the use of hydrogen fuel cells. The Boeing Fuel Cell Demonstrator plane is powered by these, set inside the airframe of a motor glider (one with an engine). This plane has flown straight and level for 20 minutes on power supplied solely by the fuel cells. It is clean, quick, and quiet.

▲ *A Super Dimona motor glider was fitted with energy cells to generate pollution-free power.*

◄ *The Lockheed LM1 is kept airborne by the helium gas inside.*

How a hydrogen cell works

A hydrogen cell converts hydrogen and oxygen into an electric current and water. Every cell has two electrodes: an anode and a cathode, separated by **electrolyte**. Hydrogen atoms enter the cell at the anode. A chemical reaction there strips them of their **electrons**, so they become hydrogen **ions**. The electrolyte won't allow the electrons to pass through it, so they flow away to form an electric current. The hydrogen ions carry a positive electric charge. They pass through the electrolyte to the cathode where they join with oxygen to form water.

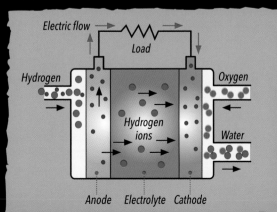

Electric flow

Load

Hydrogen

Oxygen

Hydrogen ions

Water

Anode   Electrolyte   Cathode

RECORD-BREAKERS

In 2014, Alan Eustace dropped from a balloon at 135,889 feet (41,419 m)–the highest freefall record. His descent through the upper atmosphere was very fast and he reached a speed of 821 mph (1,322 km/h) before opening his parachute.

This slowed his fall so much that he glided gently to the ground 15 minutes after cutting himself loose from the balloon. With this attempt, Alan also set the record for the highest helium balloon ascent carrying a person.

◀ After his epic adventure, Eustace falls gently back down to Earth.

▲ Alan Eustace's balloon launches from Roswell, New Mexico.

Freefall record

Felix Baumgartner became the first person to travel faster than sound while not in a vehicle, when he jumped from a helium balloon in 2012. His freefall reached a top speed of 844 mph (1,358 km/h)!

Wonderful wingsuits

Japanese wingsuit pilot Shin Ito holds the world record for the longest flight: an incredible 17 miles (27 km). And in 2016, another wingsuiter, Joe Ridler, hit a max speed of 233 mph (375 km/h).

▶ *Shin Ito achieved his record over California in May 2012.*

Longest solar flight

The longest non-stop flight by a solar-powered, fixed-wing plane was achieved by Solar Impulse 2 in 2016: a distance of 4,481 miles (7,212 km) from Japan to Hawaii in a time of 117 hours and 52 minutes.

▲ *Solar Impulse 2 on its record-breaking flight.*

Mountain jumping

Valery Rozov performed the world's highest BASE jump (that is, from a fixed structure) in a wingsuit. He leaped from Changtse mountain in Tibet, falling close to the north face of the mountain before gliding down to land on Rongbuk Glacier, almost 4,200 feet (1,270 m) below.

HIGHLIGHTS OF FLIGHT

Balloons and parachutes are probably ancient devices. But only since the 18th century have people definitely been able to use them safely. Many other forms of engine-free flight date from the last century.

1797

André-Jacques Garnerin leaped from a hot-air balloon over Paris, suspended from a parachute he had made. He hit the ground with a bump but survived.

3rd century CE

Kongming lanterns (below) were small balloons used for signaling military information in China. Candles heated the air inside them.

1485

Leonardo da Vinci sketched a design for a parachute made of cloth and tied to a square wooden frame. No one knows whether anyone tried to use it then, but the design has recently been tested—and it works!

1783

The first hot-air balloon to carry passengers, built by Joseph and Étienne Montgolfier, was flown in Annonay, France, on September 19.
The passengers were a sheep, a duck, and a rooster.

c.1600

Fausto Veranzio, an Italian inventor, may have been the first to perform a parachute jump, leaping from St. Mark's Basilica in Venice.

1894

Otto Lilienthal built an artificial hill near his home in Germany to launch his homemade gliders. A regular crowd of people watched his experiments.

1897

Percy Pilcher built a glider called the Hawk, which he flew 820 ft (250 m), a world record at the time.

1979

Bryan Allan "cycled" Gossamer Albatross across the English Channel.

1988

Daedalus 88 set the world record for a powerless plane flight when it traveled between the Greek islands of Crete and Santorini.

2014

Alan Eustace completed the world's highest-ever parachute jump.

2016

Sun-powered Solar Impulse 2 completed its flight around the globe.

GLOSSARY

airship: power-driven aircraft that is kept buoyant by a body of gas, usually helium, which is lighter than air

aluminium: a lightweight metal

atmosphere: the mixture of gases (mostly nitrogen and oxygen) surrounding Earth

carbon fiber: tough, light material made of strands of carbon

climate change: changes in Earth's weather patterns generally believed to be caused by rising temperatures from increased greenhouses gases

cockpit: compartment for the pilot of an aircraft

electron: subatomic particle in an atom with a negative electric charge

electrolyte: liquid in which electric current is carried by the movement of ions

endurance: the ability to do something difficult for a long period of time

envelope: structure that contains air or another gas

fiberglass: a strong, lightweight material

fossil fuels: fuels such as coal, oil, or gas that were formed from the remains of animals or plants in the geological past

fuselage: main body of an aircraft

greenhouse gas: a gas that helps Earth's atmosphere retain heat

ignite: to catch fire

ion: an atom with an electric charge. They are created when an atom gains or loses one or more electrons.

lift: the force produced by the movement of an aircraft in flight, which keeps it aloft

maneuver: to change direction suddenly

propane: a hydrocarbon gas (combining hydrogen and carbon atoms) used as a fuel

relief missions: operations to provide food, medicine, and shelter to the victims of famines or other disasters

synthetic: not found in nature, but made by people

▶ The LM1 hybrid airship will be able to reach those who don't live close to paved roads or runways–who make up two-thirds of the world's population.

INDEX

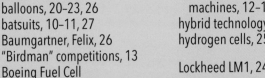

The Author

Tim Harris lives in London and loves the natural world, science, and travel. He has written many children's and adults' books for Bloomsbury, Dorling Kindersley, National Geographic, and Grolier. His subjects include the history of engineering, animal anatomy, great battles, meteorology, and geography. Tim has also edited several travel guides, and before entering the world of book publishing, he was deputy editor of *Birdwatch* magazine.

Picture credits (abbreviations: t = top; b = bottom; c = center; l = left; r = right)

1= ShutterStock. 2 =ShutterStock. 3 Solar Impulse 2. 4/5 = ShutterStock. 6/7, c = Flyfoto/Alamy Stock Photo. 8/9 = Gary Wainright/Alamy Stock Photo. 9, tr = Shutterstock. cr = US Army Photo/Alamy Stock Photo.. br = ShutterStock. 10, b = Cultura Creative (RF)/Alamy Stock Photo. 10/11 = Oliver Furrer/Alamy Stock Photo. 12, b = Peter Kemp/AP/REX/ShutterStock. 12/13 c = NASA Daedalus. 13, t = Simon Dack/Alamy Stock Photo. 14/15, c = ShutterStock. 15, tr = ShutterStock. 15, br = Thierry Grun/ Alamy Stock Photo. 16/17, c = Elijah Weber/Alamy Stock Photo. 17, bl =, ShutterStock. 17, tr = Dirk v. Mallinckrodt/Alamy Stock Photo.. 18/19 = Solar Impulse 2. 20/21, c = ShutterStock. 20, bl = ShutterStock. 20, br = ShutterStock. 22, t = ShutterStock. 22, bl ShutterStock. 22, br = ShutterStock. 23, tr = ShutterStock. 23, tl = ShutterStock. 23, b = , ShutterStock. 24/25 = Lockheed. 24, bl = Mick Flynn/Alamy Stock Photo. 25 tr = Thierry Grun/Alamy Stock Photo. 26/27, c = EDB Image Archive/Alamy Stock Photo. 26, cl = Rex. 26 bl = Rex. 27, tr = ShutterStock. 27, br = Furrer/Alamy Stock Photo.. 28/29 = ShutterStock. 31 = ShutterStock. 32 = ShutterStock